BARRON'S

Otto von Frisch

Canaries

Photography: Uwe Anders
Illustrations: Johann Brandstetter
Translated and Adapted by Matthew M. Vriends, Ph.D.

CONTENTS

TYPICAL CANARY

- **Beautiful feathers**
- **Various color mutations**
- **Domesticated and tame**
- **Lively and agile**
- **Excellent singer**
- **Clean and neat**
- **Easy to take care of**
- **Likes avian or human companionship**
- **Quiet at night**

Canaries are spirited, alert, and constantly in motion—"They couldn't be any birdier," as an acquaintance of mine said recently. To me, canaries emanate an incredible vitality. They're always cheerful and ready for action. To make sure that your bird will retain this liveliness you should ask yourself, before you go canary shopping, whether you will be able to care properly for this delightful bird.

THINK BEFORE BUYING

1 If provided with proper care, a canary can live for 10 to 14 years. Are you ready to assume long-term responsibility for it?

2 Do you have a permanent place for the cage in your apartment or house? A canary that is constantly moved from place to place does not feel safe.

3 Do you have enough time to devote to your bird? It will have to be fed and tended regularly.

4 Do you have other pets that might be dangerous to a bird? A dog can be trained to leave a bird alone, but cats usually are not that cooperative.

5 Canaries don't sing with constant fervor all year. When molting, for instance, all their energy goes into growing new plumage, and some birds stop singing for no apparent reason. Will you love your quiet canary just as much?

6 What if you want to take a vacation or have to go to the hospital?

7 Are you acquiring the canary for a child? If so, you will have to explain how to take proper care of the bird and to keep an eye on it yourself.

8 There may be veterinarian's bills if your bird should become ill. Can you afford to incur such expenses?

9 A canary should have a chance to fly free in the room every day. Will you mind if it leaves some droppings here and there?

10 *Important:* Are you sure that no one in your family is allergic to feathers or feather dust? If someone is allergic, you should not keep birds.

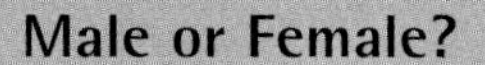

Male or Female?

I have never been able to detect any differences of character or temperament between cocks (males) and hens (females), to use the terms by which fanciers refer to their birds. I find all canaries equally lovable.

✔ Females sing less than males do.

✔ If you want a bird that sings a lot and has a varied repertoire, you should choose a male. Only males produce real songs made up of distinct parts and incorporating different musical elements.

✔ Sexing canaries is not easy because males and females hardly differ in outward appearance.

Song provides the only clue. Males sing for longer periods, and have a larger repertoire than females, which will only occasionally imitate a melody. Generally, breeders and dealers keep canaries segregated by gender. If this is not the case, ask the seller about the sex of the bird you are interested in. Since the dealer will have observed the birds over time, he or she should be able to answer this question for you.

PURCHASE AND HOUSING

The canary's popularity is based on its attractive appearance and lovely song. In our admiration for the little bird's charms we must not forget, however, that the canary requires something from us, its owners, in return: living conditions and care that take into account its natural needs.

History of the Canary

When the Spaniards conquered the Canary Islands in the late fifteenth century, they brought the first wild canaries back to Spain. There monks with an astute business sense started to breed these small, yellow-green songbirds and in time built up a thriving trade. Since they sold only cocks abroad, anyone who wanted canaries was forced to turn to the Spanish monks. During the seventeenth century, however, some Italians succeeded in breeding smuggled female canaries. From Italy, canaries spread to Switzerland and into the German and Dutch-speaking parts of Europe.

The Wild Canary

The wild relative of our pet canaries, whose scientific name is *Serinus canaria canaria*, inhabits the Canary Islands, Madeira, and the Azores. It is closely related to the European serin (*Serinus serinus*).

Appearance: The wild canary is somewhat smaller than most strains of our cage birds. The yellow color so typical of the latter is found also in the plumage of their wild cousins, but it is mixed with green, olive green, and dark brown. The females' colors are more subdued than the males'.

Habitat: Open landscapes in flat areas and on hillsides are the preferred environment of wild canaries. There they seek shelter in trees and bushes where food is plentiful.

Life pattern: The reproductive period of wild canaries begins in February or March. At this time the males begin to sing in earnest and perform ritual courtship flights. As soon as a male has found a mate, the female begins to build a nest, usually in a forked branch near a tree trunk, 6 to 9 feet (2 to 3 m) off the ground. One or two broods are raised in the course of the summer. As soon as the last fledglings have become independent, the canaries gather in large flocks and spend the winter flying from place to place on the islands in search of food.

Millet seeds are an important component of a cage bird's diet. Canaries eat them with great relish.

Breeds and Colors

There is a large variety of canaries to choose from. Breeders have increased color and type

The bird on the right is trying to shoo the intruder away from the apple.

during the many years that canaries have been kept as cage and aviary birds. However, for the neophyte bird keeper the question of breed is secondary. All canaries can sing; the only difference is in the composition of their songs.

Purebred canaries are divided into three groups:

✔ Song canaries. Breeders concentrate on producing birds with beautiful songs.
✔ Color-bred canaries. These are available in a great variety of hues.
✔ Type or posture canaries. These birds differ in shape from the original wild canary.

Ear Candy: Song Canaries

Breeders discovered early on that these cage birds had a talent for imitating the songs of other birds and incorporating bits and pieces of these songs into their own repertoire. The next step was to systematically develop the song of young canaries. These efforts have been so successful that today different strains of birds can be distinguished from each other by their characteristic ways of singing.

The Roller or Hartz Roller is no doubt the best-known song canary. Tyrolean miners originally bred these little birds and took them to the Hartz region in Germany when they emigrated there. From the Hartz, canaries were sent all over the world.

The Hartz Roller, considered the most virtuoso singer, presents its song in soft tones and with an almost closed bill. The song, which comes from deep within the throat, is free of all the impure and strident sounds that sometimes creep into the voices of other canaries. There are 14 song passages, divided into two groups: the roll (a fast drum roll) and the tour (a more emphatic beat); these musical characteristics have their own special names, such as the hollow roll, the bass roll, the flute, and the hollow bell. The Roller's repertoire also includes other notes, such as schockel, glucke, water roll, and bell roll.

The Belgian Waterslager is somewhat larger than the Roller canary and has been bred primarily in the Flemish region of Belgium. Its song is more varied than that of the Hartz Roller (its repertoire can include as many as 17 different tours), although not all parts of the song are equally mellifluous. There are some loud and harsh notes, and some tours are sung with open beak.

The American Singer is a fairly recent strain developed in the late 1930s in the United States. In this variety, a cross between a Roller and a Border canary, the song resembles that of the Roller canary. Quality of voice is not the only thing judged; beauty of color and good conformation are also important. Similar goals are pursued by breeders of a relatively new type of bird, the Song and Color canary, which, in addition to singing well, possesses attractive plumage.

A Vivid Palette: Color-bred Canaries

The common ancestor of all canaries, the wild canary (*Serinus c. canaria*), is green and yellow with black streaking and brownish black wings. Through mutations—sudden changes in the genes—and selective breeding, many color varieties have evolved over time. There are now white, red, orange, brown, silver-brown, and orange-brown canaries, as well as many other variations in color. Even so, yellow is still the best-known canary color, perhaps because yellow was the first color obtained through mutations in the course of breeding wild birds.

Color foods: Many breeders and fanciers feed their color canaries synthetic color substances during the molt to enhance certain colors in the plumage.

Warning: This practice can be harmful to a bird's health. Don't be surprised if the bright red canary you purchased turns pale after its next molt. Instead, be glad that its body rid itself of the harmful color-enhancing chemicals.

An Extravagance: Type Canaries

The breeding of so-called type or posture canaries calls for special emphasis on the shape of the birds. Breeders distinguish between small, large, curved-back, frilled, and plain varieties.

Crested canaries, such as the Gloster Fancy Corona and the German Hooded canary with its Beatle-like mop of feathers, are especially unusual looking and always fascinate

A canary often lets a partner groom parts of the body it cannot reach with its own beak.

PORTRAITS OF CANARIES

A small sampling of the colorful palette of canaries. The variety of purebred canaries is astonishing. However, the average bird lover is still most familiar with the traditional yellow canary.

Above: Softer in color: a yellow frost.

Above: A yellow crested Gloster Fancy Corona.

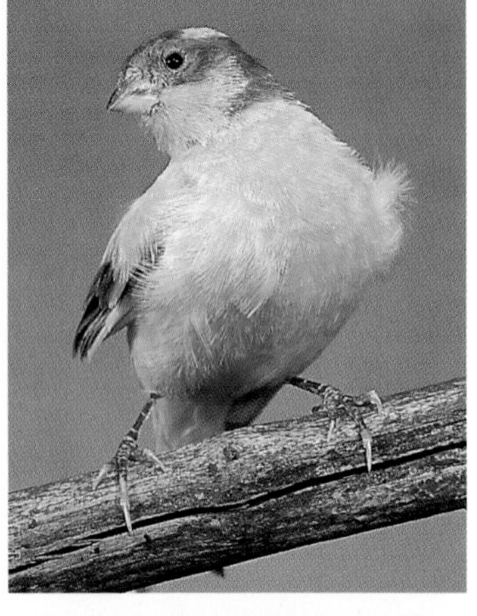

Left: This hybrid or "mule" looks very much like a wild canary (**Serinus c. canaria**).

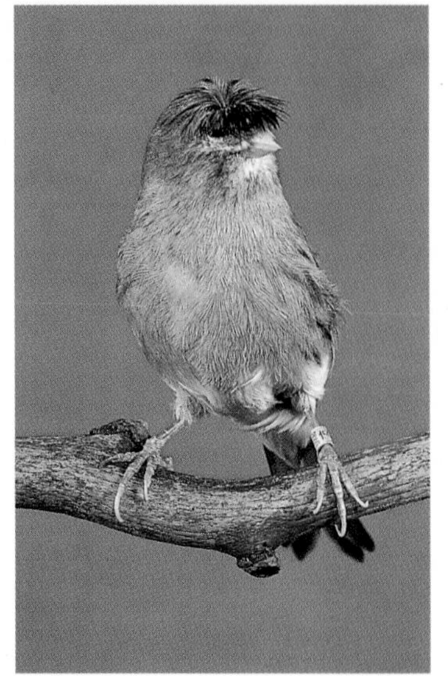

Right: A light gray Gloster Fancy Corona.

Above: Red and yellow colorbred canaries.

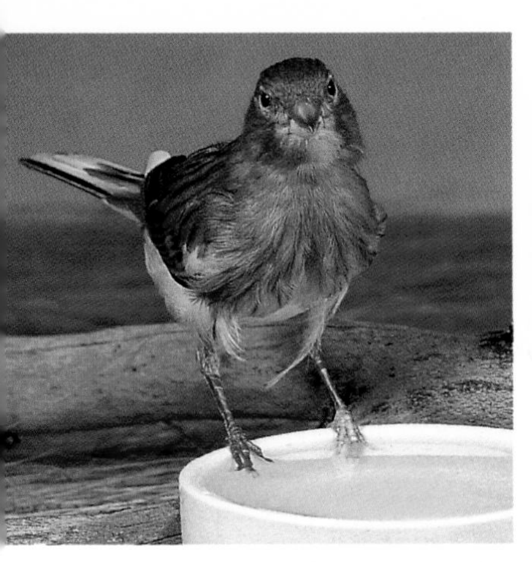

Left: This beautiful mutation looks like its wild ancestor.

Above: Left, a color mutation; right, a crossing among various color mutations.

Right: This is a yellow ground melanin canary.

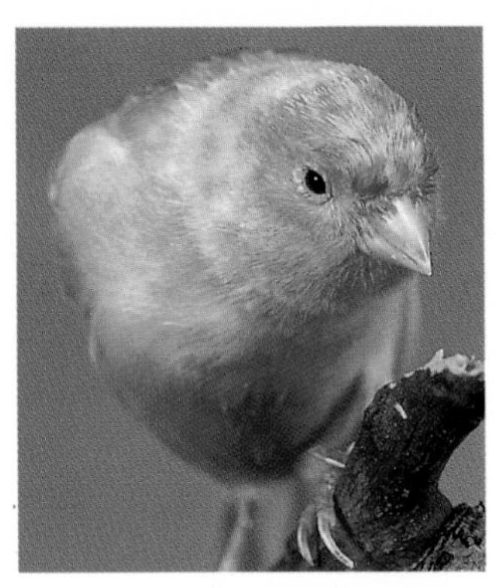

Above: Red lipochrome canary in molt or poorly colorfed.

Two yellow and one red canary relaxing on a perch. (Bird on left may be a red ground bird that has not been colorfed.)

Above: This bird is a Gloster Fancy Corona.

spectators at shows. The small "feather dusters" on their heads look very cute.

Other type canaries, such as the Bossu Belge, Gibber Italicusfrill, Scotch Fancy, Southern Dutch Frill, and Milan Frill have been bred to stand unnaturally erect, and some of them have long, frilly feathers sticking out on various parts of the body. Little remains of the original shape of a canary. In nature a bird with such impractical plumage would not survive long.

One, Two, or Several?

I cannot recommend keeping a single canary unless you are planning to devote a considerable amount of time to it. A bird that is left alone all day gets bored and lonely. However, if you are able to play and talk with it frequently in the course of the day, it will come to accept you as a surrogate partner.

Keeping a pair is ideal if you have a full-time job or are away from home frequently for other reasons. A canary is always happier in the company of others of its kind.

Generally, canaries live together peacefully even though there may be occasional harmless pecking or squabbling over food.

Keeping several canaries is possible if you have room for a large indoor or garden aviary.

Canaries are nonaggressive and can in some cases get used to living with various kinds of birds. Perhaps you already have a small avian community and would like to add a canary. Canaries can easily fit in with such birds as Diamond Doves, Superb Starlings, all kinds of finches, various cardinal species (e.g., Yellow or Green Cardinals), Senegal Doves, Pekin Robins, parakeets, and Chinese or Painted Quail. Larger birds, such as parrots, may attack the canaries, even in a large aviary.

The Song of Canaries

Canary fanciers consider their birds' song sweeter than that of any other cage bird. A canary singing at the top of its voice embodies joy in life. Of course, the singing of a bird is not at all the same thing as our whistling or singing in the shower when we are in a good mood. On the contrary, it is a male bird's way of establishing and defending its territory and attracting a female.

Analyze your expectations: Most bird lovers who decide to get a canary look forward to having a bird that will sing a lot and vocalize in varied tones. This is a perfectly legitimate desire, of course, but don't be disappointed if your new pet falls short of your expectations. Some

The yellow canaries expect a snack and the red one tells them, in no uncertain terms to clear out.

canaries, for whatever reason, are reluctant singers or suddenly stop singing altogether (see page 51). This happens now and then, and the higher the owner's expectations were at the outset, the greater the disappointment is later on.

A pitiful sight is a male canary that is kept alone in a tiny cage so that nothing will distract him from singing. Contrary to widespread opinion, male canaries also sing if they are kept in large cages and in the company of other birds. A male canary sings even if it shares a cage with a female—although not as frequently, since there is no need for it to attract a partner. To compensate for the lack of singing displays associated with courtship, however, you will be rewarded with especially varied songs during the incubation period.

If you want a singer:

✔ Take plenty of time when buying the bird, and listen to the various songs of different canaries. Some singers that are bred for attractive color have very loud and shrill voices. In the long run such a voice might grate on your ears.

✔ If it matters to you to have a canary with a beautiful voice, ask the advice of an expert who is knowledgeable about song canaries.

✔ Buy a young cock from that year's breeding. These birds have already learned to sing.

Best Time to Buy

If you want to get as young a bird as possible, autumn is the best time to look for one. At this time the greatest choice is available at pet stores and from breeders. This is the time of year when breeders get rid of young birds, wintering over only their breeding stock until the following spring. At this point the young birds are about 4 to 5 months old and have already passed through the postjuvenile molt. If you are interested in getting an outstanding singer, wait until November because it takes that long for the male's song to become firmly established.

Buy your bird in the morning, so it will have plenty of time to adjust to its new surroundings before darkness falls.

TIP

Buying a Canary

If you don't have much experience with birds, take along someone who is more knowledgeable. Allow yourself plenty of time to watch the available birds at your leisure. Ask the seller whether the bird is accustomed to having people around.

Make a health check:

✔ A healthy bird has smooth, clean looking plumage with no bald spots. Clean legs; the horny scales should form a smooth surface. The foot has 3 toes pointing forward, 1 backward. The droppings should be produced at regular intervals; they should be of a mushy consistency.

✔ A sick bird has tousled, dirty plumage with bald spots. The legs are scabby, with scales sticking out; also, toes might be missing. Birds exhibiting apathetic behavior, such as sitting on perches or floor of the cage with ruffled feathers and closed eyes are probably ill. Watch for runny droppings.

Purchase the cage and accessories and set them up before you buy the canary so that the bird will find everything in its new home ready for use. To ease the transition for your new little friend, ask to be given some of the birdseed mixture the bird is used to.

Where to Buy

Pet stores sell many varieties of canaries. You can also buy all the necessary accessories there.

Private breeders also sell canaries. Addresses are available from various canary breeders' associations (see Information, page 62).

Although this is not a common practice in North America, do not buy through mail-order firms. It is an act of cruelty to mail a bird in a tiny box where it will be frightened half to death and perhaps subjected to rough handling.

A Comfortable Cage

Even though cage canaries don't know what life in nature is like because they have been bred in captivity for generations, they, like all birds, still need plenty of physical exercise. Therefore, a canary's cage can never be too big. Free flight, of course, is possible only when the bird is loose in the room or in a large aviary (see below), but even in its cage a canary should at least be able to hop from one perch to another. Choose a large, rectangular cage for your canary. In addition to the usual metal cages with plastic bottoms, there are box cages made of wood with grating on only one side. These box cages are useful for new arrivals that are still very shy, and for sick birds. They provide peace and quiet and make birds feel secure.

The best kind of cage for your canary is made of metal and should be at least 10 inches (25 cm) high, 12 inches (30 cm) wide, and 23 inches (58 cm) long. Bigger is better, if you have room. Length is more important than height, because canaries exercise by flying back and forth, rather than up and down.

Shelves have to be cleaned frequently if you keep cages on them, so you might want to screw sturdy hooks into your wall to hold the cage or cages, creating a decorative display and eliminating your having to clean shelves. Check the hooks frequently to make sure they are securely fastened to the wall.

A seed dispenser is practical when you have to leave the bird alone for a day or two.

Cage stands: Pet stores sell many kinds of cage stands. These can be very practical for moving a bird temporarily to another spot while you clean or air its room.

Not suitable for birds are cages with unnecessary, fancy decorations. These cages are hard to clean and unsanitary. Bamboo and fancy wicker cages should also be avoided for this reason. Experienced aviarists have been advising against buying them for years.

A large flowerpot saucer is big enough to serve as a canary bathtub. Plastic bathhouses are available commercially. Most canaries love to splash.

Luxury Homes: Aviaries

Aviaries, also called flights, are spacious cages big enough for birds to fly around in. Depending on how large an aviary you have, you can keep several canaries in it or combine canaries with other small seed-eating birds (see page 28). The pet supply trade offers quite a large variety of aviaries. Ask your pet dealer to show you the catalogues of different manufacturers of indoor and outdoor aviaries. If you want to build an outdoor aviary, you can buy prefabricated parts that even people without much building experience can assemble. Before setting out to build an outdoor flight, however, you should study some of the literature on the subject (see page 62) and be sure that the climate in your area is suitable.

The accessories for an aviary are essentially the same as for a cage, but you can introduce more perches. Also, in order to prevent or reduce competition for food, you should always provide several food dishes.

The Right Location

Selecting the right spot for your canary is an important first step in assuring the bird's happiness. Not just any place in your house or apartment will do. Choose a place that will not have to be changed later on, since a bird familiarizes itself with its new surroundings from the perspective of its cage. Like all birds, canaries are

creatures of habit, and any change is perceived as a threat.

This is what the canary's habitat should be like:

✔ It should be as quiet as possible.
✔ It should offer the bird a good view of the room so that it can watch everything that is happening there. The cage should be placed at about eye level on a shelf, stand, or wall bracket.
✔ It must be absolutely free of drafts, which can make canaries ill. Check for drafts with a lit candle; the flame will flicker at air movements you might not even be aware of.
✔ It should be bright (near a window) but not exposed to direct sunshine.
✔ There should be no temperature fluctuations. A canary's reserves of body heat are quickly used up.

Whetting the beak helps keep its horny surface clean. It is important that birds have natural branches available for this purpose.

✔ The space above the cage should be empty. Canaries get frightened if anything goes on above them.
✔ A relative air humidity of 50 to 70 percent is ideal. Excessive humidity combined with heat can lead to heatstroke, and cold dampness makes birds susceptible to sickness.

The following locations are unsuitable:

✔ The kitchen. If the kitchen is drafty, fluctuations in temperature are created. Also, the air humidity changes often in a kitchen. For a canary, these changes can result in colds, pneumonia, hoarseness, and even total voice loss. Never let your bird fly free in the kitchen.

✔ A spot too close to a television set. Television emits tones in the ultrasound range that are audible to birds and are perceived by them as very shrill. The bird should be at least 10 feet (3 m) away from a TV set. (If you keep your canary in a room away from the TV and other evening activity, you won't have to cover its cage at night.)
✔ Rooms in which people smoke a lot.
✔ Locations not completely free of vibrations. Birds are very sensitive to the slightest tremors. The oscillation of a refrigerator motor, for example, can be very frightening to a bird. Never put the bird down in such a spot even for a minute.

Replacing the Perches

Most canary cages are equipped with ½-inch (12 mm) thick perches made of plastic or hardwood. This uniformity of size forces the bird always to use the same grip, a situation that can, sooner or later, lead to foot problems. Natural branches of various thicknesses provide much more exercise for a bird's feet and toes and thus keep them fit. Also, the rough surface of twigs and branches helps wear down the claws properly. For these reasons you should replace the commercial perches—at least some of them—with natural branches. Immerse branches in boiling water for ten minutes to kill any insects or eggs that might have come in on them, and then let them dry thoroughly. Place some horizontally, others at an angle. Wild birds landing on swaying tree branches don't always end up on a horizontal perch. Make sure, however, that no perch is mounted too close to the grating of the side walls; otherwise the bird's tailfeathers will keep rubbing against the bars.

Suitable branches are those from unsprayed fruit trees (except cherry) and from other deciduous trees such as birch and willow.

Checklist
A Well-Equipped Cage

1. Ideally a cage should measure approximately 40 inches long, 20 inches wide, 32 inches tall (100 × 50 × 80 cm).
2. Perches should be made of wood of varying thickness, from ½ to ⅝ inch (12 to 16 mm).
3. Baths are essential for birds and should be placed in the opened cage door or on the floor.
4. You need three dishes: one for birdseed, one for fruit, and one for water.
5. Line the bottom tray with newspaper and change it daily.
6. Fill a dish with mixed birdseed, and fill a cup or bottle with water.
7. Hang a millet spray near one of the perches.
8. Insert a cuttlebone or a calcium stone between the bars of the cage.
9. Replace commercial perches with natural branches that have been sterilized by immersing them for 10 minutes in boiling water.

HOW-TO: COMING HOME

The Trip Home

Once you have chosen your canary, it will be handed to you in a small cardboard box with airholes. Get your canary home as quickly as possible, taking care not to expose it to heat, dampness, drafts, or cold. To make the transition easier for the bird and to minimize adjustments, the cage should be all ready for its occupant, with full food and water dishes, and set up in its permanent place. If you have to adjust things in the cage after the canary is in there, you—or your hands—may become associated, in the bird's mind, with everything that is strange and unpleasant.

Your canary will be comfortable in this type of cardboard carrying box.

Place your hand near the food source.

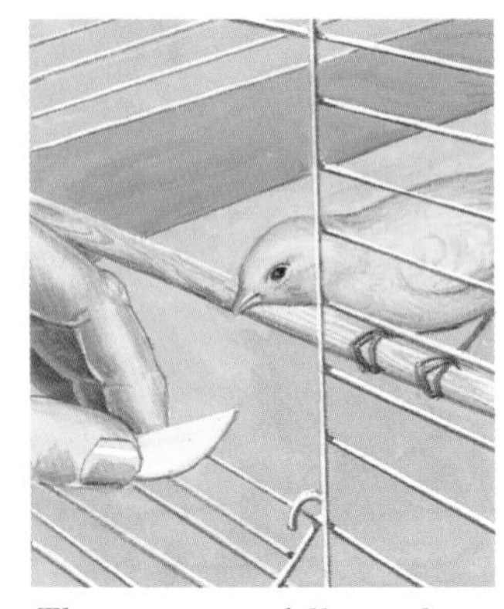

The canary carefully reaches for the food.

At last the bird will trustingly perch on your finger.

Hand-taming Your Canary

✔ Don't try to approach the bird until it has become used to its new situation. It should have reached the point where it remains calm and no longer flutters around nervously when you are doing things near the cage.

✔ Then you should be able to reach your hand slowly through the open cage door and offer the canary a piece of fruit.

✔ If the bird gets nervous, withdraw your hand slowly.

✔ Always talk to the bird, so that it can get used to the tone of your voice.

✔ Be patient, and keep offering treats.

✔ Once the canary has accepted your hand as the bearer of treats, it will soon hop onto the back of it or onto an outstretched finger.

✔ Never grab your bird.

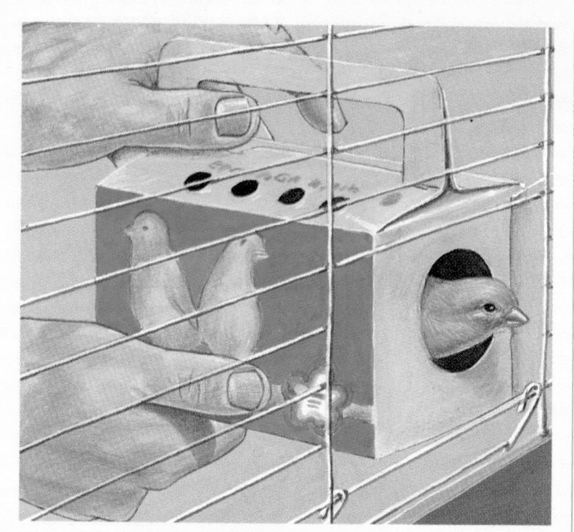

Don't try to take the bird out of its box. If the bird refuses to come out, place the box on its side, with the cover open, on the floor of the cage.

The First Few Exciting Hours

When you get home, hold the cardboard box next to the cage door and open the cover. Make sure there is no crack between the box and the door through which the bird could escape. Glad to get out of its dark prison, the canary will probably hop toward the light. Now slowly close the cage door and move away from the cage. You will, of course, be curious and eager to watch, but give the bird some time first to familiarize itself with its new surroundings.

Important: Remember, even hand-tame canaries hate being grasped (see page 49).

Night Rest Is Important

Like all birds, canaries like to have an undisturbed night's rest. It is a good idea to drape a light cloth over the bird cage around 8 P.M. You can leave the radio or TV on later, as long as the sound is not turned on too high. Birds in the wild are used to night sounds. What is more important is that your bird not be startled suddenly at night, as by the light being turned on.

Canary Temperament

Some canaries accept a new cage without seeming ill at ease; others act frightened. Some begin to sing soon after they move in; others utter only a shy little "peep." You can soon tell which type your bird is. If it fluffs up its feathers, preens itself, and eats and drinks soon after arrival, it is the self-assured kind. If, on the other hand, it acts nervous, fluttering around and making itself look slim—a typical fear posture—or huddles motionlessly on a perch, then it is still afraid. If the latter is the case, keep away from the cage, though you may stay in the same room and talk soothingly to the bird.

What frightens birds

- ✔ A sudden change in appearance, as when you put on a hat, glasses, or an unfamiliar item of clothing
- ✔ Hasty movements
- ✔ Being grabbed
- ✔ Abrupt changes in the bird's immediate environment. Even having a food dish moved to a new place is upsetting.
- ✔ Loud, excited voices
- ✔ Unfamiliar people

It takes patience and love to make a bird hand-tame.

LIFE WITH A CANARY

Canaries do not by nature have the same need for closeness with people or other birds as do some other cage birds. Canaries seek partners only for the duration of a breeding cycle and go more or less their own ways the rest of the time. Still, it is possible to get these little birds so accustomed to your presence that they lose their natural fear of the human hand and become hand-tame.

Flying Free—Heaven on Earth

Every cage bird should have a chance to use its wings fully, as often and as long as feasible. This exercise strengthens the circulatory system and builds muscles. But wait until the bird is thoroughly familiar with its cage, recognizing it as the place for eating and sleeping and as a safe haven, before you let it out to fly. If you grant it freedom too early, it may refuse to return to the cage.

The first time: You will probably be puzzled if your bird refuses to take advantage of the open cage door. This reaction is not so surprising, however, if you remember that this may well be the first time the bird has been offered a chance to fly. Until now it probably could do nothing more than flap its wings. Just be patient; at some point the urge to fly will overcome fear. Never chase the bird out of the cage. To do so would badly shake its confidence in the cage as a safe haven.

An aid for taking off and landing: For a bird still unused to flying, taking off and landing can present problems. Flying through the small door opening is a challenge in itself and one that hardly any bird will manage on the first try. For this reason you should set up a perch about a hand's width from the cage and on a level with the cage door sill. This perch will not only be of great help for taking off and returning to the cage but also serve as a resting place.

The return to the cage: If your canary shows no inclination to return to the cage, just leave it where it is, even overnight. Hunger and thirst will eventually motivate it to return.

Important: Never chase the bird or try to move it by waving a towel at it. One way to encourage it to return is to feed it only inside the cage.

The canary's vision is monocular; the two large eyes function independently of each other. Birds have a very large field of vision (320 degrees in canaries).

Favorite Spots

Canaries like high perches because, in nature, being high means being safe from predators. If you want to do your bird a favor, therefore, put up some branches in the upper part of the room, making sure to attach them securely. Pet stores sell clamps for this purpose. Firmly established perches have the added advantage that you can spread newspapers underneath, which will catch most of the bird droppings. No bird can be toilet trained, and you will have to be prepared to do some cleaning up after your canary. Of course, your bird may spurn the offered perches and find its own resting places.

The Dangers of Free Flying

All doors and windows must be closed before your canary flies free. But even with closed windows a little bird can be exposed to some dangers that you might not be aware of.

Dangers in the room: Take a good look around the room where the bird will fly, trying to see it from an avian perspective. Are there some potential landing sites that are so smooth that your canary might slip, such as a tabletop or the rim of a flower vase, or some electrical appliances that are sometimes hot, such as the burners on a stove or a toaster? A search for crumbs on a sofa can end in disaster for a bird if it is not seen there and is sat upon. Unfortunately, such mishaps are not rare.

The dangers of a window: Birds that are afraid—and almost any bird is filled with fear on its first free flight—automatically fly toward the brightest light; in a house, this is toward the window. Light to them suggests the safest escape route, and your canary, which has no way of knowing that there is an invisible but solid barrier between it and the freedom outside, will in all probability crash against the window glass.

Keeping the curtains drawn is the best way to prevent such accidents. If there are no curtains or shades, a sheet should be hung in front of the window. This precaution is necessary at other times, too; for example, when the bird might slip out of its cage while you are cleaning it. It is, therefore, a good idea to have a screen in the window of the bird's room. Then you can leave the window open even while the bird is flying free.

Enough food for two? Don't take chances—defend what's there!

Dangers for Your Canary

Source of Danger	Accident	Protect Your Canary
Bookshelves	Bird may slip or fall behind the books and get stuck there.	Push the books flush against the wall.
Windows, glass walls	Birds may crash against them and suffer a concussion or skull fracture.	Keep curtains drawn or lower shades during free flying.
Containers of water (glasses, vases)	Bird may slip in and drown.	Cover. Take vases out of the room while bird is loose.
Poisons: Alcohol, chemicals	Fatal poisoning.	Keep these things where bird cannot get at them. Wash off all traces.
Stove burners, open pots	Bird can burn itself if it lands on a hot burner or be scalded or drown in a pot of hot liquid.	Be sure all burners are turned off and are cool. Never let bird fly free in the kitchen unattended.
Candles	Bird can burn itself.	Do without candlelight while bird is loose in the room.
Open windows and doors	Bird may escape or be crushed by a closing door.	Keep doors and windows closed during free-flying sessions, and tell others in the family that bird is out of its cage.
Open drawers and cupboards	Bird may be shut in unnoticed and suffocate or starve to death.	Shut everything before letting bird out of the cage.
Wastebaskets, ornamental vessels	Birds may slip in and starve to death or suffer heart attack.	Use woven baskets, or line the inside with wire mesh so bird can climb out. Fill ornamental vessels with sand.
Sun	Bird may suffer heatstroke if cage stands in full sun.	Make sure there is shade.
Spaces between walls and furniture	Bird may slip down and get stuck.	Keep an eye on bird while it is flying free.

10 House Rules

1. New canaries are always nervous and shy. Children should be introduced gradually to a canary and to taking care of it.

2. Children have to be taught to approach the bird quietly and gently, and not to touch it at first.

3. Place a little lock on the cage door so small children can't open it.

4. Keep children quiet when the canary is flying free in the room.

5. Children should clean the canary's cage only under adult supervision. The same rule applies when children are taking care of the bird's food and drinking water.

6. Children are not allowed to hold the canary. It could have a heart attack.

7. Keep children's toys away from the canary. It might be frightened by them. Let the bird get used to the toys and everything else in the room gradually.

8. Make clear to children that even a canary needs its rest and privacy.

9. Always explain to children the essential rules regarding proper care and management.

10. Children quickly lose interest. Supervise them as they care for the bird. Realize that you might end up taking care of it yourself.

Hazardous plants: Make sure that all plants in the bird's room are nonpoisonous, in case your canary decides to nibble on them.

✔ Poisonous house plants: Poisonous primrose, *Strychnos nuxvomica*, catharanthus, crown of thorns, all *Dieffenbachia* species, yew, hyacinth, periwinkle, all nightshades, narcissus, oleander, berries of *Ardisia* plants, poinsettia, variegated laurel, the berries of ornamental asparagus, rosary pea, caladium, elephant's ear, and azalea.

✔ Plants with substances that irritate the mucous membranes: Ivy, *Monstera*, flamingo flower, Chinese evergreen, philodendron, and Schefflera.

✔ Cacti and plants that have thorns or spiny parts (possibility of eye injuries).

Fresh Air

Fresh air and sunlight are as important to canaries as their daily session of free flying.

Spring and summer: If you can, let your bird spend some of its time on your balcony or in your yard—safe in its cage, of course. Find a draft-free, partially shaded spot, as under a tree. But don't forget that there may be cats around. Always stay nearby and keep an eye on the cage. If you are lucky, you may see your canary make contact with other birds. One canary owner reports that when she placed the cage on her balcony, her female canary was visited for several days in a row by young greenfinches. Five of them sat on the cage roof, fluttering their wings and begging for food. And lo and behold: the canary fed the fledglings seeds from morning till dusk, completely absorbed in this unanticipated maternal task.

During winter: Unfortunately some people keep canaries in rooms so overheated that the birds can barely breathe. Too little humidity in the air dries out the mucous membranes and makes birds, like people, more susceptible to colds and other illnesses. Having plenty of plants (note the list of dangerous ones on page 24) in the room helps raise the air humidity, particularly if they are plants with fleshy leaves, such as begonias, that need a lot of water. Humidifiers made of unglazed clay that hang on radiators also help. If you keep your living room at a moderate temperature, that is, about 64–68°F (18–20°C), and frequently let in some fresh air (without creating drafts), both your own and your bird's health will benefit. On cold nights, when the heat is down, keep your windows closed.

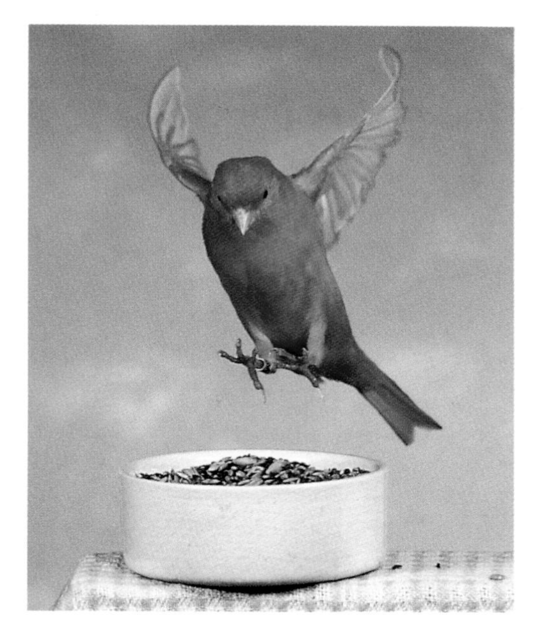

A red-factor canary comes in for a landing.

Escape Artist

Even when the weather is mild, a canary is not likely to live long outdoors. For one thing, its bright color makes it an easy target for any predator, whether it be the neighbor's cat or a

CANARIES ON VACATION

When you go on vacation you have to make plans not just for yourself but also for your bird.

Vacations abroad are out of the question for canaries because entry regulations applying to cage and aviary birds are so stringent.

A trip by car is possible, but if the canary goes along, you have to make sure there are no extremes of temperature between an air-conditioned car and hot weather. If you stay in a hotel or motel, the bird has to stay inside its cage to prevent its escape.

Staying at home is the best alternative for the bird.

Ask a friend or relative to look after the bird and talk to it twice a day. Give written instructions and leave a phone number where your canary sitter can reach you.

Sometimes pet stores or veterinary offices board birds for a small fee.

Wherever you leave your bird, always have enough of its familiar food and toys available.

bird of prey. In addition, a cage bird is not used to foraging for its food; in the cage it always had a full food dish.

An escaped canary is terrified by its unfamiliar surroundings. Usually it heads for a nearby tree. If you can spot it there, keep watching it and talking to it, for as long as it is still in the vicinity there is hope it will return.

What you can do:

✔ Place the cage on the windowsill or balcony.

✔ Sprinkle some food in and around the cage.

✔ If the bird is on a low branch, try to capture it with a bird net.

✔ If you don't know where the bird is, put an ad in the local paper saying that your canary has escaped and perhaps offering a reward for its return.

What you should not do:

✔ Run after the bird in a panic, let alone climb the tree after it.

✔ Call the fire department. Most fire departments will not commit their firefighters and equipment to something they consider unimportant. Even if they respond, by the time the firefighters set up their ladder, the canary will have moved to another tree.

Canaries and Other Pets

Birds, especially small ones, have an instinctive fear of not only larger birds but also furry animals. There is a good reason for this reaction, for fur-bearing mammals such as cats, dogs, foxes, martens, and weasels prey on small birds in nature. This doesn't mean that you can't get a canary if you already have a dog. A dog can be taught, with a little ingenuity and adequate patience, that the bird cage is off limits. Still, you should never leave bird and dog in the same room unattended, even if your dog always keeps a respectable distance from the cage in your presence. Keeping a bird in the same household with a cat is more problematic. Cats are avid hunters, and the constant presence of forbidden prey is very frustrating for a cat. Should the cat so much as reach a paw into the cage, the bird will suffer excruciating fear. To train your dog or cat to stay away from the cage, zap it with water from a squirt bottle every time it approaches the canary's territory.

A Canary with Other Birds

If you are going to introduce your newly purchased canary into an indoor or outdoor aviary with other birds, don't add the newcomer to an already established bird community without careful planning. A group of birds that have been living together in an aviary for some time can make life miserable for a new arrival. They know where food and water are available; they claim certain spots for perching, resting, and sleeping; and they have—especially if there are pairs—their established territories.

TIP

Moving with a Canary

Moving seldom presents a problem with canaries. After all, the bird keeps on living with you in its familiar cage; only the surroundings change. If you had perches in the bird's room in your former house or apartment, try to provide similar perching opportunities in the new one. No pet bird likes its surroundings changed. For this reason you should take the bird out of its old quarters before you start removing the furniture and should put it in its assigned spot in the new home only after all the furniture is in place there.

An argument over some fresh lettuce.

A newcomer to the community knows none of these things. The whole scene, including the other birds, is completely unfamiliar. The new bird is frightened and shy. It has to learn where to find food and water and where it may be allowed to rest. In most cases it won't have a chance to look for these necessities in peace because the other birds will chase it away as soon as it approaches their territories or tries to settle down in a spot claimed by another bird. In nature this wouldn't be a problem because the new bird could get as far away as necessary. But in an aviary, with its limited space, the situation could end in tragedy. Sometimes a new bird is attacked by the others so persistently that it no longer dares approach the food dish and after a few days falls over dead from hunger and exhaustion.

Safety Precautions

✔ Never introduce a new canary into a community aviary during the breeding season. At this time birds are particularly territorial.

✔ Start out by putting the newcomer in a small cage, stocked with food and water, which you then place in the aviary for a few days. From this safe vantage point the canary can gradually become familiar with its new environment.

✔ A more complicated procedure involves catching and removing the established birds and housing them somewhere else for a few days, thus giving the new canary a chance to adjust to the aviary in peace. When you return the old-timers, however, watch carefully for a few days so that you can intervene if there are any fights.

The Daily Bath

Canaries love to splash in water. Since they enjoy bathing, and it keeps them healthy, you should let your canary have a bath every day. Fill the bath about 3/4 inch (2 cm) deep with water, and hang it in the opening of the cage door. The best time for a bath is in the morning, so the plumage can dry thoroughly by evening.

The water: Because birds often drink as they bathe, the bath water should be as clean as the drinking water. Tap water that has been left standing for a while is fine. The water should be no more than lukewarm; if it is too warm, it washes away the oily substances that make the plumage waterproof (see page 48). Also, birds that bathe in water that is too warm may catch cold easily because the water heats their damp skin, making it more sensitive to drafts and cold. Water that is too cold can, of course, also result in colds.

Your canary may regard the bath skeptically at first. After all it is a new, unfamiliar object that it has to get used to. Hang the bath in the door opening every day. If you wish, you can place some washed parsley, tender dandelion greens, chickweed, or spinach leaves in the bottom. Some birds like to get themselves just a little wet

This canary is testing the water.

Regular Chores

Frequency	Chores
Daily	Empty all dishes and the water bottle. Wash them in warm water, dry them, and refill them (the seed dish only half full). Change paper in bottom of cage. Offer fresh water for a bath. Check to make sure that food and water dispensers are working properly and are securely mounted, that the cage doors lock properly, and that no bits of rotting or moldy food are stuck in corners or cracks.
Weekly	Clean the cage or aviary, including accessories (wash with warm water, then dry well). Scrub dirty perches with a perch scraper or sandpaper and wipe them with a damp cloth. If the aviary has a dirt floor, rake it thoroughly; flagstones or similar floor materials should be washed.
Monthly	Disinfect the cage or aviary and accessories; use 1 tablespoon of bleach in a gallon (3.8 L) of water. Replace branches (see page 19).
Every three months	Thoroughly spade the soil in an outdoor aviary. Check the wire mesh for holes and rusty places; don't forget the lock.

Maintaining sanitary conditions in a cage or aviary is of prime importance. Even if you are sometimes short of time or don't feel like doing chores, just remember that your bird has the same right to clean dishes and sanitary surroundings that you have. In fact, its health and life depends upon it. Your best bet is to draw up and adhere to a schedule of maintenance tasks (see above).

Important: Don't use any chemical cleansers or rinses when you clean. The ingredients in them are toxic for birds. The water should not be any hotter than about 130°F (55°C).

by playing with fresh greens. Wash lettuce thoroughly, because it is usually sprayed to get rid of pests.

If your bird doesn't want to bathe: There are canaries that stubbornly ignore the bath. This doesn't mean that they are afraid of water or dislike it. In fact, they are probably desperate for a bath but can't overcome their distrust of this mysterious plastic box. Perhaps they don't like the color, or maybe the location seems unsafe. If the bath is hanging in the door opening, the bird has to step outside its safe cage to bathe. If you think that is the problem, put the bath on the cage floor. If that doesn't help, try spraying the bird cautiously with water from a plant mister. Some canaries thoroughly enjoy this shower, turning around to expose themselves at all angles (see page 50).

Seed as the Basic Staple

A well-balanced birdseed mixture, preferably with some supplemental commercial pellets, constitutes the bulk of a canary's diet. A good mixture consists of niger and canary grass seed (also called white seed), with small amounts of rape, hulled oats, and hemp, and perhaps some poppy seed, wheat kernels, lettuce seed, various millet varieties, and linseed.

Important: The grains and seeds should be as fresh as possible. For this reason you should not buy too much birdseed at a time and should check to make sure the packing date on the box or bag is not more than 3 months old. To make sure that the food is still fresh, you can test the viability of the seeds by sprouting them (see page 34). Only seeds that still sprout are high in nutrients. If only a small percentage sprouts, the mixture is useless and should not be fed to the bird.

Seed Test:

✔ Decay: Rotting seeds have a penetrating odor; fresh ones don't smell.

✔ Mold: A whitish gray film on some of the seeds means that the food is moldy.

✔ Vermin: Seed clumps and cobweblike filaments indicate the presence of vermin.

Proper storage: Birdseed should always be stored in a dry, cool place. Plastic bags or metal cans with lids may be stored in the refrigerator after they have been opened.

Fruit, Vegetables, and Fresh Greens

Fruit, vegetables, and greens are indispensable parts of your canary's diet and provide variety in the menu. Your bird will no doubt refuse some of the things you give it; tastes vary among birds, just they do among people.

Fruit: Apples, bananas, berries, pears, honeydew melon, kiwi fruit, tangerines, sweet cherries, watermelon, grapes.

Vegetables: Fennel, cucumbers, potatoes (cooked), kohlrabi, grated carrots, radishes, soybean sprouts, zucchini, broccoli.

Greens: Basil, endive, corn, daisies (without the stems), garden cress, grasses (especially annual bluegrasses), shepherd's purse, coltsfoot, chervil, lettuce,

Won't you join me in a slice of honeydew melon?

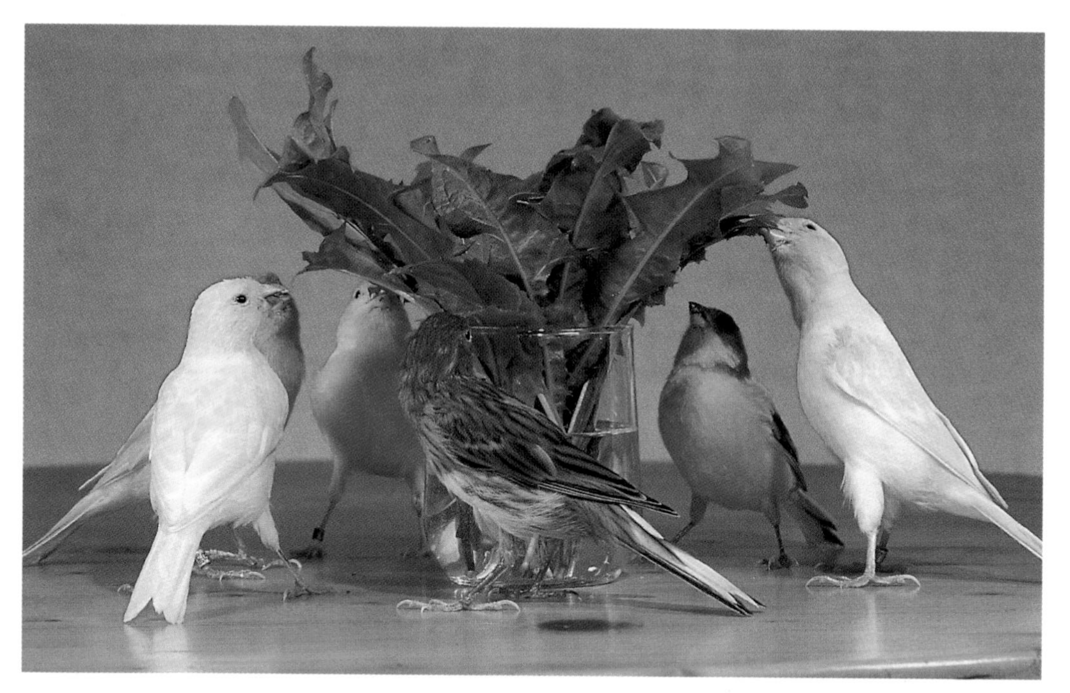

ragwort, dandelion greens, parsley, dock, spinach, knotweed, chickweed, plantain, vetch (leaves and flowers).

Things to Add to the Bird's Menu

Vitamins: Bird vitamin supplements are available from pet stores. Dribble the drops on the birdseed or add them to the drinking water.

Minerals and trace elements: The most important of these—calcium and phosphorus—are present in mineral stones given to birds to whet their beaks on, as well as in bird sand. Cuttlebone is also a good source of calcium. Cuttlebone should be placed so the *soft* side is toward the bird.

Fresh twigs: Fresh willow, birch, or fruit tree branches, together with cuttlebone and mineral stones, are excellent for keeping the beak in good shape.

Dandelion is high in vitamins. Bring home a small bunch for your bird when you are out walking. Be sure that the area has not been sprayed with pesticides or that fertilizers were not used, and wash carefully before giving your canary its treat.

Spray millet: Attach a millet spray to the cage bars or put it in a holder especially designed for this purpose.

A home-cooked treat: Hard-boiled egg yolk mixed with some low-fat cottage cheese is a good source of protein.

Drinking Water

Canaries need fresh drinking water every day. Let tap water stand for an hour or two to allow any chlorine to dissipate.

Important: Change all water daily.

HOW-TO: FEEDING

The Right Amount of Food

There is no magic formula that tells you how much to feed your bird. The amount of energy your canary expends depends to a large degree on how much it is allowed to fly and whether it is going through a physically demanding period such as molting or raising young. Rely on trial and error. If the bird ravenously attacks the food you give it in the morning, you can assume that it was hungry.

Cucumber is excellent for canaries.

Ten Important Feeding Tips

1. Feed a varied diet.
2. Give fresh food only.
3. Give moderate amounts of food at regular times.
4. Offer only as much fruit and greens as will be consumed within one day.
5. Avoid sudden changes in diet.
6. Don't give anything directly from the refrigerator.
7. Don't collect wild plants along the roadside (exhaust fumes!), from meadows frequented by dogs (bacteria in the dogs' urine or feces) or from locations too close to agricultural fields (possible pesticides).
8. Supply fresh drinking water daily, perhaps with a vitamin supplement.
9. Make sure the bird always has a mineral stone or cuttlebone available.
10. Always offer soft food in a separate dish.

Sprouting Recipe

✔ Cover ½ teaspoon each of birdseed, oat kernels, and wheat kernels with ¾ inch (2 cm) of water and soak for 24 hours.

✔ Rinse the seeds with lukewarm water and let drain; then place in a glass dish and let sit lightly covered for 48 hours at room temperature.

✔ As soon as sprouts appear you can give them to the bird. Rinse them with lukewarm water first and drain well.

Important: Sprouts get moldy quickly. Throw away any sprouts that have not been eaten after about 2 days.

Only birds that are hand-tame will trustingly perch on the food dish.

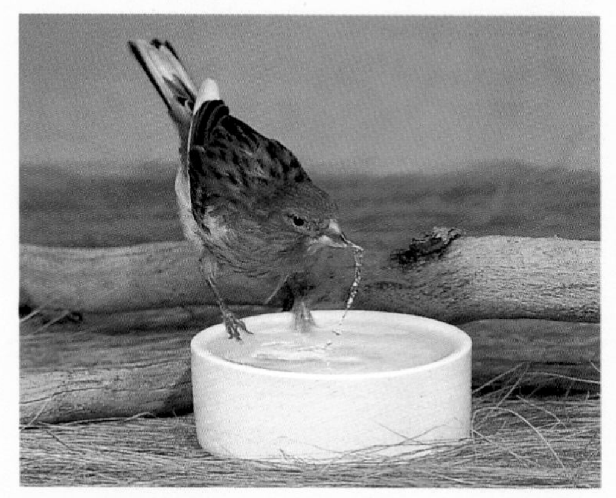

Fresh drinking water should always be available.

How to Feed Fruits and Vegetables

✔ Depending on the consistency, cut fruits and vegetables into pieces that can be stuck between the cage bars.
✔ Attach small bunches of greens to the cage roof with a clothespin or other clamp.
✔ Offer perishable foods in the morning. Remove what is left in the evening.
✔ Have fruits and vegetables at room temperature when given.
✔ Wash everything carefully in warm water and pat it dry before giving it to the bird.
✔ Keep in mind that the juicier the food, the less you should give at a time.

Foods and Drinks Harmful to Birds

Tame or free-flying canaries often like to join their human families at mealtimes. If no one minds having a bird at the table, there is nothing wrong with this. Taboo for birds are
✔ Salty or spicy foods; pure salt, spices, and sugar
✔ Chocolate and other sweets and candies
✔ Cream, butter, cheese, and other fatty foods
✔ Alcoholic beverages and coffee

Various fruits are an important component of a canary's diet and are eaten by the bird with great relish.

Menu Plans

How Often	What Kind of Food	How Much
Daily	Birdseed mixture Fruit, vegetables Millet spray	Approximately 1/3–1/2 oz. (10–15 g) 1 small piece 1 spray hung in cage until it is eaten
Every 2 or 3 days	Sprouts Soft food	Approximately 1/3 oz. (10 g) Approximately 1/3 oz. (10 g)
Once a week	Fresh twigs (see page 19) Hard-boiled egg yolk with low-fat cottage cheese	Unlimited 1/2 teaspoon

Raising Baby Birds

The best way to assure that a pair of canaries will go through the reproductive cycle undisturbed and produce healthy offspring is to isolate them in a cage of their own.

How to Find a Mate

The breeding season for canaries starts in the spring. If you don't have a pair yet, start looking for a mate for your bird in the fall. The pair will have all winter to become acquainted with each other. However, don't let the new bird join its future mate right away! Keep the two in separate cages at first, but have them close enough that they can see and hear each other. Then gradually move the cages closer together; or, if you have an aviary, move the cage with the new bird closer to it.

By no means can it be taken for granted that two canaries will

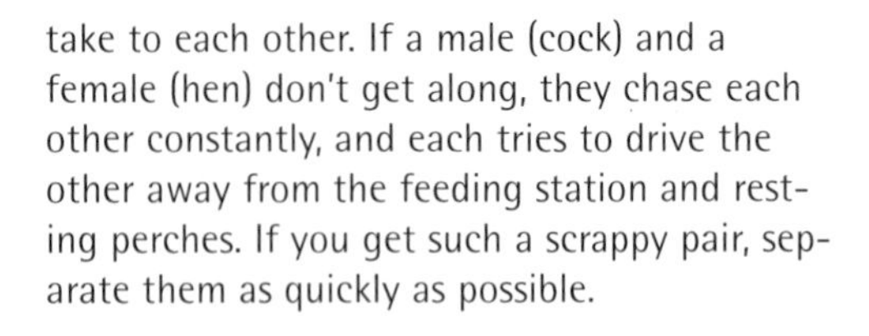

take to each other. If a male (cock) and a female (hen) don't get along, they chase each other constantly, and each tries to drive the other away from the feeding station and resting perches. If you get such a scrappy pair, separate them as quickly as possible.

Nest Building

Nest baskets: These are available from pet stores in sizes ranging from 3 to 5 inches (8 to 13 cm) in diameter. Hemispherical baskets made of woven plant fiber, wire, or plastic are readily accepted by canaries. Smooth-sided baskets don't work as well because the nesting material doesn't adhere.

Nesting materials: The availability of suitable nesting materials arouses the female's enthusiasm for brooding. For this reason you should supply a variety of nesting materials of different textures to make the nest tight and solid. Good items for this purpose are cotton thread cut into short lengths (a bird can get caught in long threads and may strangle), coconut fibers, sisal fibers, hay, dry moss, soft grass clippings, and burlap cut into 4-inch × 4-inch (10 cm × 10 cm) pieces and unraveled. Birds in outdoor aviaries often find and incorporate small feathers, fine grass stalks, and all kinds of plant fibers.

Don't offer a large amount of nesting material all at once because you never know just when a female is ready to start building, and the materials will get dirty. A few cotton threads suffice for determining at what stage the birds are.

Egg Laying

As soon as the hen has finished her nest she lays the first egg.

Canaries in love will delicately touch each other's beaks.

This almost always happens in the early morning. The hen generally rises on her legs to push out the egg, standing in the nest with her beak open. Then she settles down again exhausted and rests. With some birds, however, you can hardly tell when an egg is being laid. Sometimes the female suffers from egg binding (see page 58).

Your responsibility: It is important that you be aware when the first egg appears because this is when the bird needs your help. Wild canaries don't start sitting on the eggs until the clutch is complete. In our domestic birds, however, this instinct has been lost, and female canaries almost always begin to brood immediately after the first egg is laid. Since four to six eggs are usually laid, one a day, the baby birds will hatch at different times. As a result, the oldest nestling may be five days old by the time the last one emerges from its shell. These latecomers have little chance of survival because they can't compete with their bigger siblings for food, and they may even be crushed by them. For this reason, all of them should hatch on the same day if possible. Therefore, remove the eggs each day as they are laid, and don't return them to the nest for incubation until the clutch is complete. To move the eggs you should use a small spoon and proceed with extreme caution. Tiny eggs are very fragile. In order not to upset the laying process you will have to substitute artificial or dummy eggs made of gypsum or plastic and available at pet stores, for the real ones. The latter should be stored in an open box with a soft lining, kept from being shaken or bumped, and protected from heat and cold.

Checking the first eggs.

Incubation

The female canary usually broods the eggs by herself without help from the male. She leaves the nest only briefly in the morning and

These two youngsters are about nine days old.

evening to deposit feces and to drink. The rest of the time the male feeds her with food from his crop. Most canary hens brood very reliably. The exceptions are usually nervous birds or young and inexperienced females whose brooding instinct is not yet fully developed. Such a bird may abandon the eggs in the middle of the incubation period. The only way to try to prevent this is to make sure that the environment surrounding the cage is quiet and peaceful.

If a female turns out to be consistently unreliable as a brooder or in rearing the young, you should replace her.

Egg check: Starting on the fourth day of incubation you can, if you wish, check to see whether the eggs are fertile. Hold each egg up to the light, using a flashlight or a regular light bulb. Pick up the eggs gingerly; the thin shells will not stand much pressure. The embryo shows up as a dark spot in fertile eggs, and you can also see the fine red blood vessels. Infertile eggs are evenly translucent. The female should be allowed to sit the full length of the incubation period—about 14 days—even on an infertile clutch, to prevent disruption of the natural process. If it turns out, however, that a pair keep producing infertile eggs, you will have to replace the male and, if that doesn't help, then the female.

Hatching

After an incubation period of 13 to 14 days, the baby birds hatch. They chip a tiny hole in the shell from the inside, using the egg tooth, a small protuberance on the upper mandible.

After "pipping" the shell, the chick gradually enlarges the hole. Finally the hatchling exerts pressure with its entire body and pops off the cap of the shell at the blunt end of the egg. Naked except for a few down feathers, with large and protruding closed eyes, its lies there, its beak hungrily open.

Family Life

The baby birds are kept warm by the mother's body heat. The parents start feeding them the day after they are born. On the first day they don't need any food because nature provides them with a yolk sac that is pulled up into the abdominal cavity the day before hatching. The father provides food for the young. Often he will feed them directly with predigested food regurgitated from his crop. The mother keeps the nest meticulously clean, eating the nestlings' droppings, which are enclosed in a thick mucous fecal sac, or carrying them out of the nest. The nestling period lasts about 16 days.

Cautious Nest Check

Up to the fourteenth day you can examine the nest now and then without worry. After that, leave the nest alone. Up to this point the baby birds respond to intrusions by crowding together and hunkering down deep in the nest cavity. Now, however, their flight instinct is awakened. In an attempt to get away from your large hand they may leap out of the nest.

Special Feeding Tips

✔ Give the female calcium supplements. Laying a clutch of eggs drains the body of calcium.
✔ Give plenty of soft rearing food (available from pet stores). Parents that are feeding young should have access to it throughout the day. Make sure the food is of the right consistency; it should be light, moist, and crumbly.

Checklist
Canary Birth Control Methods

1. **Normally, canary females are broody only from spring into early summer, reflecting the natural reproductive pattern of wild birds, which raise one or two broods a year.**
2. **Domesticated birds, however, can lose this natural rhythm and remain broody beyond this time. Since more than two broods per year is too much of a physical strain for the hen, you should prevent additional egg laying after the first or second brood.**
3. **One possibility is not to let the hen build a nest. Simply do not provide any nesting material.**
4. **Many hens, however, respond by plucking their own or their mate's feathers.**
5. **In this case, let the hen build a nest and lay eggs. Remove each egg as it is laid, and substitute a dummy egg or two. The hen will sit on these eggs until she gets tired of sitting.**
6. **Then you can remove the eggs. You don't have to worry that the hen will suffer stress.**

UNDERSTANDING YOUR CANARY

Anyone wanting to satisfy a canary's natural needs has to learn to understand the behavior patterns of these birds. This chapter is meant to help you gain such an understanding. In addition to acquainting you with your canary's most important anatomical features, it will explain some motivating factors behind the bird's behavior.

Feathers: A Perfect System

Functions: It is common knowledge that down and feathers keep you warm. Birds maintain their body heat by manipulating their plumage. You can watch this behavior in your canary. If it gets too cold, it puffs up its feathers so that more air is trapped in the plumage. The air warms up to body temperature and forms an insulating layer. If the canary gets too warm, it pulls its feathers flat against the body, pressing the air out and thus getting rid of its "insulation." The plumage also hides unevennesses in the body surface and gives birds their necessary streamlined shape. And, finally, birds couldn't fly if they didn't have feathers.

Types of feathers: Bird feathers are of three types: down feathers, contour feathers, and flight feathers. The primary function of down feathers is to provide warmth; contour feathers give birds their streamlined look; and flight feathers are necessary for maneuvering in the air.

Canaries try to intimidate each other with raised wings and wide-open beaks. Such conflicts usually are just for show.

Substance: Feathers, like hair, claws, and horns, are composed of keratin, which consists of protein molecules. This substance gives the feathers their great strength and elasticity.

Why Canaries Can Fly

There are several reasons your canary can fly. Almost all the anatomical and physiological features of a bird contribute directly or indirectly to its ability to fly. The most crucial features are

A light skeleton: The bones of a canary are strong yet light and, in part, hollow. Even the wide bill contains more air than is apparent from outside. The heavier parts of the anatomy, especially the flight and leg muscles, are located next to the rib cage and the spinal column.

The lungs: The lungs of birds are extremely efficient and are able to absorb oxygen from the air even at great altitudes. Air sacs, which are extensions of the lungs, are located between the large flight muscles and other body parts. They serve primarily for cooling, so that the muscles don't overheat when the bird flies. The air sacs take up as much as one fifth of the volume of a bird's body, thereby decreasing the overall body weight and enhancing

First the breast and head feathers are carefully dipped in the water . . .

flight; the air sacs act like balloons, counteracting the pull of gravity.

A high rate of metabolism: Flying uses up a lot of energy. The high speed at which a canary can burn up food and turn it into energy is very important for flying. It has been calculated that flying requires about 15 times the amount of energy used during resting.

Further Anatomic Details

The toes: We walk on our ankle (tarsal), arch (metatarsal) and bottom of the toes (phalanges). The canary's ankle and arch bones do not even touch the ground. Birds walk and stand on their phalanges or toes.

The upper and under beak: Both have sharp edges, which replace the teeth of a mammal. They are made of bone and are covered with keratin, the same insoluble protein that gives strength to our fingernails and the nails of canaries and other birds. Since bone is a living organ, the bill continues to grow. In general, the edges of the beak are worn away at the same rate that new bone is formed. This is the reason that the bill remains the same size and shape.

The tongue plays an important role in getting, manipulating, and swallowing food. Since the ability to taste is not very well developed in canaries and other finches (in contrast with parrots), the tongue is probably not very important in food selection.

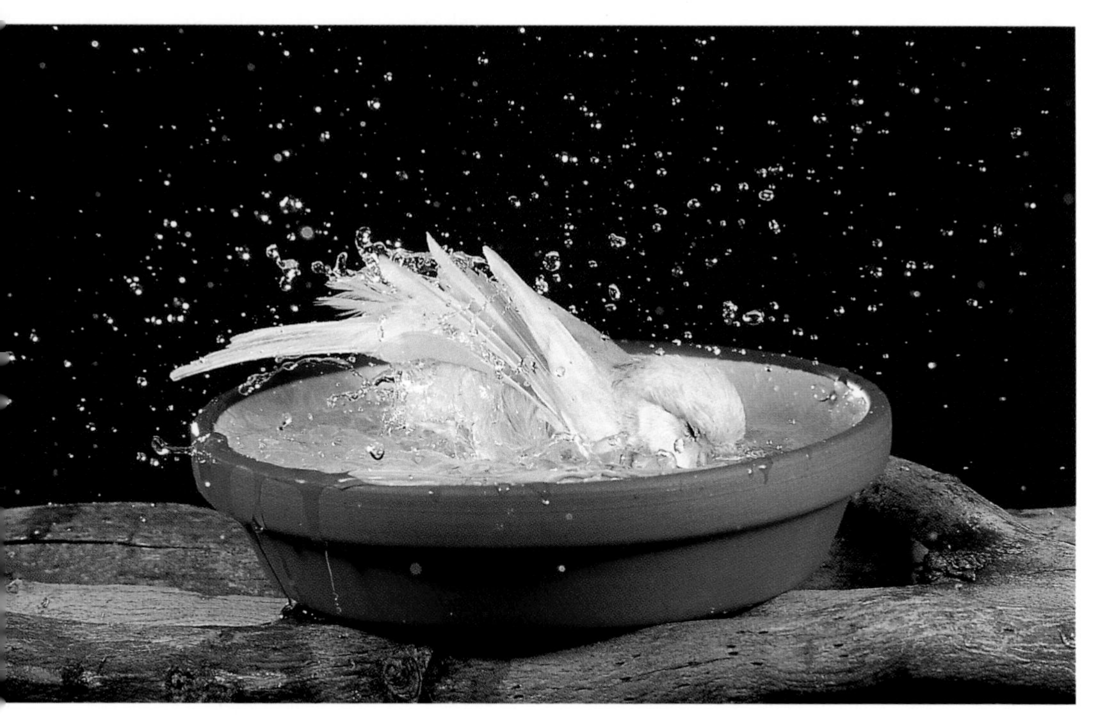

. . . then a few vigorous beats of the wings take care of the back.

Sensory Capacities

Vision: The eyes are by far the most important sense organ of birds, which orient themselves primarily by sight. Their vision is monocular; the two large eyes function independently of each other. Birds have a very large field of vision (320 degrees in canaries). The eyes of birds are also quite mobile; but whereas the human pupil can move from side to side in the lid opening, the pupil of a bird always stays in the middle. To close its eyes, a bird raises its lower eyelids.

Hearing: Birds have an acute auditory sense. In its basic structure, a bird's ear resembles the ear of a mammal, but there is no outer ear flap.

Smell: This sense is poorly developed in birds and seems to be of little consequence.

Taste: Taste doesn't play much of a role in the sensory activity of canaries and other finches.

Courtship and Mating

In early spring the canary hen begins to get restless and emit a frequent warbling call. At a later stage it is common for her to pick up feathers in her beak (the nest-building ritual). The male, meanwhile, sings at great length and feeds his mate. Sometimes he performs a dance. All this is part of the courtship display. This fairly lengthy prelude is followed by copulation, which lasts only one or two seconds. For mating, the female squats on her perch. The male jumps onto her back, crosses tails with her, and presses his cloaca against hers. Then the birds separate and usually engage in extensive preening.

UNDERSTANDING BEHAVIOR

Canaries express their feelings to other birds and humans with their pronounced body language.

 ***Behavior my canary is exhibiting.***

 ***What is my canary saying?***

 ***What should my response be?***

The canary scratches with its toes.

This is part of its daily preening ritual.

If its scratching becomes frantic, it might be infested with parasites. Consult your avian veterinarian.

Two birds touch each other's beak.

This is the correct way to establish social contact.

A singleton should have a companion: You!

The bird pecks under its raised wing.

It is caring for its flight feathers.

Offer the bird a clean cage and enough room to fly free.

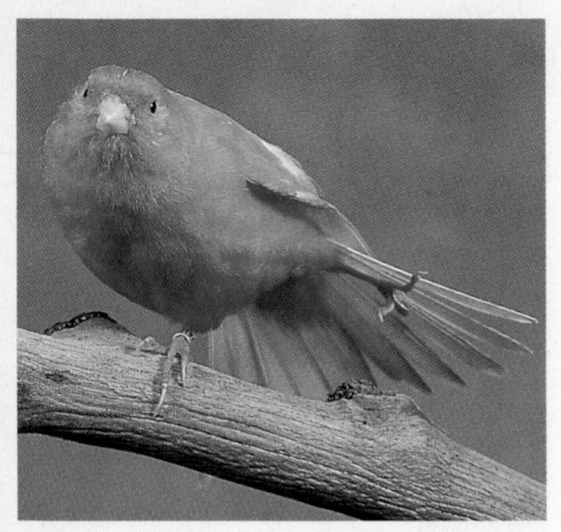

The canary stretches its body and extends its wings.

This is part of the bird's daily exercise, or it is becoming overheated.

Never place the cage in the sun or too close to a heat source.

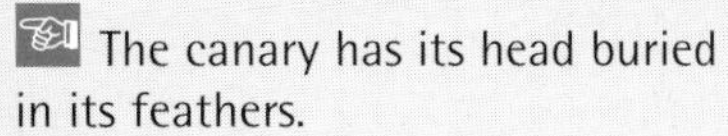

The canary has its head buried in its feathers.

The bird is either sleeping, sick, or molting.

Watch carefully for signs of sickness!

The bird sits on its perch with puffed feathers but looks content.

This is a sign that the bird feels content and happy.

Follow a schedule to maintain proper care and management.

Your canary tilts its head and looks at you.

It wants your attention.

You have to talk to your bird, and scratch its neck carefully with your finger.

The canary rubs its beak and head against its perch.

It wants to clean its beak and keep it in proper shape.

Clean and disinfect perches regularly, and supply cuttlebone.

Your bird is splashing enthusiastically, scattering water everywhere.

It feels very happy and content.

Give the bird the opportunity to bathe on a regular basis.

How Canaries Sing

Perhaps you have noticed that your canary assumes a certain posture for singing. It raises its head high and its throat swells. These actions have to do with the fact that the sounds are produced in the windpipe. As far as we know, birds can produce sounds only when exhaling. Yet a singing Roller canary sounds as if it goes on forever without pausing for air. One reason is that a bird can inhale a great deal of air, taking breaths so quickly that they are hardly noticeable. Songbirds can take about 20 breaths per second.

Another characteristic of the respiratory system of birds is that fresh oxygen can be absorbed not only during inhaling but also during exhaling.

Could this basket be right for a nest?

The Function of Singing

The frequency and the persistence with which male canaries sing tend to make us forget the real purpose of their singing. The beauty of their song fosters the illusion that canaries are musical performers wishing to please their owners. The truth is, of course, that in nature the singing is addressed to other canaries. The twofold motive of the male canary's song is to lay claim to its territory and to attract a female.

Claiming territory: A male canary claims a certain territory and advertises the fact, among other ways, by singing. In the wild, usually the singing is done from a tree or bush, but in spring birds also sing while they fly over their territories. The European siskin is one wild bird that exhibits this behavior.

Courting a female: A female that is getting ready to brood is attracted by the song of the male. If she finds him and his singing pleasing, she will join him for the length of the breeding season.

Providing an accompaniment to nest building: Canary females go about the business of nest building with much greater enthusiasm when a male accompanies their activities with song. This is true even if the song emanates from a tape recorder. In general, older, more experienced cocks have larger repertoires of songs than younger ones.

Can Females Sing?

Female canaries sing rarely and so softly that they are often not heard at all. But they have the necessary organs and physiology for singing. All they lack is the male sex hormones, which account for the frequency and intensity of the male's song. This was shown conclusively by an

Body Language of Canaries

What the Bird Does	What It Means
Spreads its wings	Threatening gesture toward other canaries or simply stretching and cooling down
Sits on one leg	Sign that the bird is relaxed and feeling well
Puffs up its plumage	Expression of comfort, but can also be a sign of illness
Opens its beak (pants)	Threatening gesture, but can also mean that the bird is feeling hot
Opens its beak wide	In young birds, request to be fed
Hacks with its beak	Sign of aggression
Hides its head in its plumage	Sleep posture, expression of relaxation and comfort, but can also be a sign of illness
Tilts its head	Invitation to be scratched by the partner, or inspecting something with one eye
Mutual preening	Feelings of empathy between the two birds
Whets its beak	Cleaning activity, but can be a mollifying gesture toward other birds
Rub their beaks	Sign of great affection between two birds
Shakes its plumage	Attempt, after grooming or bathing, to arrange the feathers properly, or a sign of relief after tension (pain or fright)
Shakes its head	Expression of disgust
Stretches its body, lifting its wings	Sign of being hot, need to cool down
Stretches its body, laying the feathers down flat	Sign of being very frightened; gesture of submission
Dances	Courtship display to impress a female

A Gloster Corona threatens a red-factor canary that dares to approach the food.

experiment that H. Voss conducted. He gave a canary hen a daily shot of androgen, a male sex hormone. After 12 days the female began to sing, at first hesitantly and with pauses, but as time went on, more frequently and with more assurance. Finally, she produced the typical "rolls" of canary cocks and even assumed a cock's posture, which is otherwise not seen in hens. She raised her head high when singing, turning it from side to side, and raised her throat feathers. This behavior lasted as long as the bird got hormone shots. When these were discontinued, the song became less frequent and less intense until the bird fell altogether silent again.

How Canaries Sleep

Birds are diurnal; they are active during the day and sleep, usually soundly, at night. Wild birds cannot afford to sleep during the day because a predator would quickly take advantage of such unguarded moments. Caged and protected by human owners, canaries can, of course, take a nap now and then during the day, and experience has taught them that this is safe. Such daytime naps, however, are always brief.

When a bird prepares to sleep it usually fluffs up its plumage somewhat, turns its head backward 180 degrees, buries its head in the back feathers, and closes its eyes. The feathers are fluffed up to keep the body warm, and one leg is often drawn up close to the abdomen. A mechanism involving muscles and tendons in the legs prevents birds from falling off their

perches while asleep. When the knee and ankle joints bend, a tendon automatically keeps the toes locked around the perch or branch on which the bird is resting.

Shows of aggression, which can arise even between birds that generally live together peacefully, usually have no serious consequences.

How a Canary Grooms Itself

The bird preens with the beak and claws, sometimes with acrobatic contortions of the body. It grasps one feather at a time with the tip of its beak and carefully puts it into place. With its toes, it scratches parts of the body that its beak cannot reach—the nape, throat, and top of the head. In order to scratch in these places, it lifts one leg with the wing of the same side slightly extended so that the leg can pass between body and wing. Ethologists call this "scratching from behind." All songbirds scratch their heads in this way, but some other birds scratch "from the front"; instead of spreading the wing, they raise the leg up past the folded wing. It is interesting to note that birds never scratch their backs or bellies. It draws the long wing and tail feathers through its beak one at a time.

To keep the feathers supple and as water resistant as possible, the canary oils them with a fatty substance from the preen or uropygial gland located at the base of the tail.

Bending its head backwards, the canary extracts a little of the gland's secretion and distributes it over the feathers.

HOW-TO: SPECIAL CARE

How Canaries Learn to Sing

The call notes and songs of many birds are totally inborn or instinctive. Other birds are born with a certain repertoire of songs but learn new ones during their nestling days and shortly thereafter, normally imitating the male parent, which is near the nest. Canaries belong to the second group. This means that a male canary can sing perfectly well—even if it is kept singly—provided that it listened to its father's singing at the crucial early age. Even if it didn't, the young bird will still sing in typical canary fashion, only perhaps with not quite so much variety.

Musical training: Once the young cocks are old enough, breeders keep them in large cages or flights, where they start practicing their songs, eagerly trying to outdo each other. Then, after the postjuvenile molt, the young males are placed singly in song cages, where each can "study" and improve its song privately. This phase lasts two months.

A tall piece of furniture or bookshelf can become a favorite landing spot and perch for your birds.

Some Prefer a Shower

Some canaries stubbornly ignore the bath. Try cautiously spraying the bird with water from a plant mister. Some canaries thoroughly enjoy this shower, turning around to expose themselves at all angles. If you use this method, the water should be warm, about 77°F (25°C), because sprayed water feels cooler. If your canary reacts with fear, stop for the time being.

Important: Make sure the spray bottle has never been used with plant sprays or other chemicals.

It is crucial for a bird's survival that its plumage always be clean and in good order. Only in this way can it maintain its full flying capacity.

If Your Canary Stops Singing

Don't be surprised if your bird suddenly stops singing during molting season (see page 56). Growing new plumage consumes so much energy that little or none is left over for singing. Sometimes this break in singing lasts longer than the molt. Occasionally a bird falls permanently silent. What can you do?

Here are a few tricks that may put your bird back into a singing mood:

✔ Play tapes or CDs of canary songs for your bird.

✔ Play music on the radio or on your stereo. Many canaries want to drown it out and therefore sing as loudly as they can. Running the vacuum cleaner sometimes has a similar effect.

✔ If you have more than one male, keep them in different cages where they can't see each other.

Branches with buds, leaves, and blossoms provide variety to your canary's habitat.

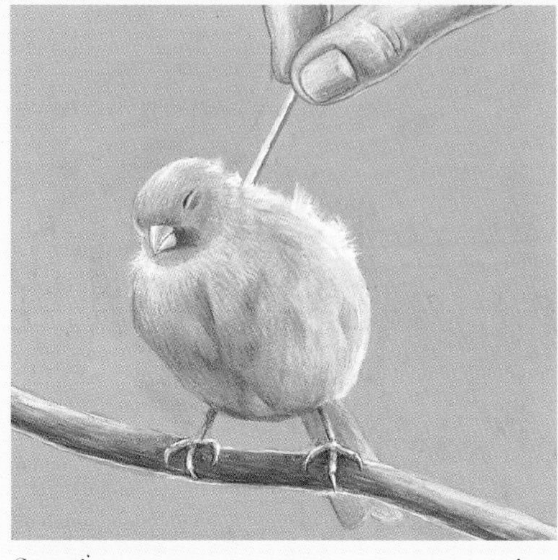

Sometimes you can encourage your canary to sing by scratching it gently with a small stick.

Avoid Boredom

Natural branches of various thicknesses provide much more exercise for a canary's feet and toes than the cage perches, usually of one size, available in pet stores. The rough surface of twigs and branches helps wear down the claws properly. Use unsprayed fruit tree branches and branches from deciduous trees, such as birch and willow.

IF YOUR BIRD GETS ILL OR IS INJURED

Proper cage and aviary care and management will prevent your bird from getting sick, but it is important to know what a healthy canary looks like. Don't hesitate to take the bird to your avian veterinarian if it shows any sign of illness.

Prevention Is Better than Cure

This principle holds especially true in the case of canaries, for, unfortunately, even an illness that seems quite insignificant can be a serious threat to these small birds. The smaller an organism is, the sooner its energy reserves are used up. Once a canary is weakened by sickness, its overall health can decline very quickly.

What can make a canary sick:

✔ Drafts
✔ Direct exposure to the sun
✔ Frequent moves from one room to another
✔ Too much noise and activity
✔ Air humidity that is either too high or too low
✔ Stale or smoke-filled air
✔ Sudden major changes in temperature
✔ Inappropriate diet, spoiled food, not enough vitamins and trace elements
✔ Contaminated drinking or bath water
✔ Lack of exercise
✔ Unclean conditions
✔ Infections
✔ Accidents

A fatty substance from the preen gland at the base of the tail keeps the canary's feathers supple and water resistant.

Recognizing Disease

If you spend time with your bird every day, you should notice if its behavior suddenly changes. A canary that is sick or just not feeling up to par will sit with its plumage puffed up. Such a bird often keeps its eyes closed during the day, hides its head in its back feathers, and doesn't eat properly. These are the first signs that something is wrong. Runny droppings, a nasal discharge, and labored breathing are more specific symptoms indicating diseases of the digestive or respiratory system.

First aid: At the first sign of sickness, you should take the canary as quickly as possible to a veterinarian with experience in treating birds. If this can't be done right away, place the cage in an absolutely draft-free, dark spot, drape a light cloth over it, and expose the bird to an infrared heat lamp (see page 54). Then leave the little patient in peace; too much fussing will only upset it unnecessarily.

Important for Aviary Birds

Birds that live in an aviary should be watched even more carefully than a single bird in a cage because a sick bird can easily infect all the others. If you notice a bird that doesn't seem well, catch it and move it to a cage of its own, such as a quarantine or hospital cage (see below). The bird may be only temporarily indisposed, but it's better not to take any chances. It is often difficult to tell whether a bird is just napping for a little while or not feeling well. If in doubt, speak to the bird, saying something like, "Well, what's the matter with you?" In response, the bird will usually wake up and fly off unless it really is sick.

The Quarantine Cage

If you house several birds together and one of them gets sick, it is best to move the patient into a quarantine or hospital cage. A box cage with a wire mesh front works well for this purpose, offering the bird sufficient peace and quiet and making it feel less exposed. The cage should have a removable tray at the bottom; by lining this tray with white paper towels or newspaper, you can keep a daily check on your canary's digestion.

Make sure there are several perches so that the bird can choose between sitting close to the heat source from the infrared lamp or avoiding it. Keep the cage with the sick bird away from the other birds, or the patient will get agitated. As a precaution, leave the canary in its separate cage for a few days even after it is well again, and check it frequently.

Infrared Heat Lamp

Exposure to an infrared lamp often helps restore a sick bird to health.

How to do it: Set up a lamp with a 150–240 watt infrared bulb about 16 inches (40 cm) away from the cage in such a way that the rays shine into only half of the cage. With this arrangement, the bird can get out of the direct heat if it wants to. The temperature in the cage should be about 95–104°F (35–40°C). Place a pan with steaming water near the cage to increase humidity. The food and water should be in the cooler part of the cage; otherwise, they will get too warm and no longer be palatable. At first birds usually puff up their plumage and settle down in front of the lamp to get warm. As they begin to feel better, they start moving farther away from the lamp. At this point you can gradually move the lamp farther away from the cage, thus lowering the temperature in the cage. Even when the heat lamp is no longer necessary, you must make sure that the temperature stays even and avoid all drafts.

How to Give Medications

When your avian veterinarian prescribes the use of drugs, please observe his or her direc-

After sleeping or sitting still for some time, canaries stretch their wings and legs.

Health Problems at a Glance

Symptoms	Possible Cases	Possible Diagnosis: Required Treatment by Avian Veterinarian
Eyelids stuck together; watery or pus-containing discharge	Drafts; smoke-filled room; infection	Eye disease
Dragging wing; inability to fly; favoring one leg	Collision; fall	Bruise or fracture
Runny droppings for longer than 1 or 2 hours	Food or bath water that was too cold; agitation caused by change in surroundings	Diarrhea or enteritis
Encrustation on legs and toes; horny scales are rough and stick up	Unclean conditions: dirty cage floor and perches; mites	Foot disease or scaly leg (common in canaries)
Lack of appetite, diarrhea	Infection	Many possibilities; visit to avian veterinarian mandatory (take along a sample dropping in a jar)
Restless sleep; constant preening and searching through plumage; sneezing	Infestation with red mites, or air sac mites	Mites; infection
Long molt (more than 4-8 weeks); feathers are brittle and dull	Wrong or unbalanced diet; abrupt temperature changes or temperature extremes; changes in light periods; shock or severe fright; hormone imbalance	Molting difficulties
Apathy; bird sits around with puffed up feathers, tries to pass droppings	Food that is too old; ingestion of foreign bodies; inability to expel an egg that is ready to be laid	Constipation or egg binding (the latter can occur in a female kept singly)
Claws too long; bird can no longer perch properly and gets toes caught in things	Perches that are too smooth and thin	Have claws trimmed by the veterinarian or your pet dealer

TIP

Visiting the Veterinarian

If your bird's behavior doesn't return to normal within a few hours, you should take the canary to an avian veterinarian. If you keep it in a cage that can be transported, leave it in its familiar quarters. Place clean white paper towel in the cage bottom so that the veterinarian can check the consistency of the feces accurately and easily. A bird from an aviary is best transported in a small cardboard box with air holes punched into it. Protect the bird from cold, moisture, and heat on the way.

Questions the veterinarian may ask:

✔ How old is the canary?
✔ Where did you get your canary?
✔ When did it first look sick to you?
✔ What, specifically, did you notice?
✔ Has the bird ever been sick before?
✔ If so, who treated it, and what methods and medications were used?
✔ What birdseed mixture (or pellets) does it eat? (Take along a sample.)
✔ What does the bird drink?
✔ What fruit and vegetables has it been eating?
✔ Could it possibly have nibbled on something poisonous?
✔ What other animals live in your household?
✔ Do you keep it with other birds?
✔ Where in your house do you keep it?

tions to the letter. Only the veterinarian can decide what medications are appropriate and how often they should be given.

Vaccinations for Aviary Birds

There are two dangerous contagious diseases against which canaries living in outdoor aviaries should be vaccinated.

Canary pox: This disease is transmitted from bird to bird and by bloodsucking insects. Unfortunately it is quite widespread, attacking canaries as well as related birds such as sparrows and finches. Have your canary inoculated against the virus when it is at least 3 months old, assuming that it is healthy and not molting at the time. Don't let the bird bathe for three weeks after the vaccination.

Newcastle disease: The virus of this disease is either introduced through raw egg shells or transmitted by wild birds. Ask your avian veterinarian about preventive vaccinations.

Molting: Change of Plumage

Bird feathers are quite fragile. By the time they have been in place for a year, they show signs of wear and tear. For wild birds it is a matter of survival to have plumage that is in tiptop shape. For this reason the feathers are replaced at regular intervals by means of a process called molting (from the Latin *mutare*, to change).

Although the molt is obviously not a disease, it is discussed here because canaries are susceptible to disease during molting. Don't be surprised if your bird stops singing at this time. This is only natural, since growing new plumage taxes the entire physical system.

Timing of the molt: Because of the strain it places on the organism, molting is carefully alternated with other times of physical exertion in the annual cycle of a bird's life. Like birds living in the wild, your canary will molt in June

Three different colors of canaries: Left, Gloster Corona; center, red lipochrome and right, yellow lipochrome (both colorbred).

through September, depending on the temperature in your home or aviary. They do not molt during the breeding season. There may be a rare winter or spring molt, during which only the small feathers are replaced. The new plumage will grow in within six to eight weeks.

If your canary loses its feathers during the molting season but doesn't grow new ones, or if the replacement of the feathers takes unusually long, nutritional deficiencies and hormonal imbalances are likely causes.

How you can help the molting bird:

✔ Treat the canary especially gently. Birds are often abnormally nervous at this time.

✔ Feed it an especially wholesome and nutritious diet with vitamin supplements.

✔ Give some unwaxed cucumber peel or small pieces of cucumber. Cucumbers seem to aid the process of feather formation.

✔ Offer the bird a chance to bathe daily or spray it with a plant mister.

✔ Expose it to an infrared lamp daily (see page 54).

Egg Binding

If the female puffs up her feathers and sits around motionless, she may be suffering from egg binding. This means that an egg that is ready to be laid cannot be expelled. Several causes can account for this situation. If a normally developed egg cannot be laid, the female might be sick or weakened. More often, however, the problem is that the egg lacks a hard outer shell. An egg without a calcium shell does not respond to the pressure of the muscles that should move it down the oviduct. A hard shell will not form if, for instance, the female did not get enough calcium before the laying period. Egg binding also occurs in females that are too young for breeding.

Important: If you are a novice breeder, take a canary suffering from egg binding to an avian veterinarian. Only experienced aviarists should attempt to try the various methods of dealing with this condition.

Tips for experienced bird keepers:

✔ Expose the female to an infrared heat lamp (see page 54).

✔ Place a drop of warm salad oil in the cloaca with an eye dropper. This often provides the necessary lubrication, and the egg is expelled within a half hour.

✔ Massage the area around the cloaca very lightly and carefully. An egg without a shell can be broken open in this way and will then practically flow out of the cloaca. A normally formed egg, however, must not be crushed because the pieces of shell can cause internal injuries.

✔ You can also help matters by dipping the lower part of the hen's body in alternating cool and warm water baths.

✔ Placing the patient in a hospital cage with a temperature of at least 85°F (30°C) usually helps, too. If not, carefully hold the hen above steaming water, after first placing some salad oil on the cloaca. Don't expect the egg to come out the first time; often it takes several efforts before success is achieved. Once the egg has been laid, the patient should be kept in the "infirmary" for at least three more days. Maintain normal room temperature and provide a variety of foods.

The sharp beak rips off pieces of fresh leaf.

Ornithosis

This disease is hard to diagnose because its symptoms aren't clear. If, however, your canary suffers for an extended period from lack of appetite or weight loss, shortness of breath, watery green droppings, sniffles, or slimy discharge from the eyes, you should consult the veterinarian. Ornithosis (called psittacosis in parrotlike birds) can be transmitted to humans by infected birds. However, treatments have been developed that, if begun early enough, are effective for both humans and birds. Because any incidence of ornithosis can pose a hazard, you are required to report any suspicion of the disease to a veterinarian or the U.S. Public Health Service.

Fresh fruit should be an essential part of the canary's daily diet.

INDEX

When the others aren't looking, their cagemate sneaks a snack.

INFORMATION

National Canary Associations

American Canary Fanciers Association
Ralph R. Tepedino, president
213-255-2679

American Norwich Society
Will and Lee Burdett, treasurer and secretary
113 Murphy Rd.
Winter Springs, FL 32708

American Singers Club Inc.
Clayton C. Beegle, treasurer and secretary
Rt. 1, Box 186
Ridgeley, WV 26753-9718

Central States Roller Canary Breeders Association
305 Grosvenor
Bollingbrook, IL 60439

Hartz Club of America
2719 S. Komensky
Chicago, IL 60623

National Gloster Club
58 Joanne Drive
Hanson, MA 02341

National Colorbred Association
Bob Metheny
236 Lester Street
Burleson, TX 76028

National Institute of Red Orange Canaries
Ellie Merriman
P.O. Box 93
Mokena, IL 60448

National Norwich Plainhead Canary Club
743 Pasadena Place
Milford, OH 45150
www.anglefire.com/fl/Norwich canary/

Stafford Canary Club of America
George E. Gay, president
687 Westvaco Road Highway 51 S.
Wickliffe, KY 42087

Internet List Group

Canary-List
http://members.aol.com/CanaryList/index.htm

Bird Associations

American Federation of Aviculture, Inc.
P.O. Box 56218
Phoenix, AZ 85079-6218

Avicultural Society of America
P.O. Box 5516
Riverside, CA 92517

International Fife Fancy
11614 January Drive
Austin, TX 78753-7116

International Gloster Breeders Association
1816 Twigg Rd.
Ferndale, WA 98248-9302
b.rosario@juno.com

North American Border Club
36051 S. 545 Rd.
Jay, OK 74346
brammer@greencis.net

Old Varieties Canary Association
4147 Fuqua
Houston, TX 77048

Books

Vriends, Matthew M., *Simon & Schuster's Guide to Pet Birds*, 10th edition; Simon & Schuster, New York, New York, 1998.

___. *Hand-feeding and Raising Baby Birds*, Barron's Educational Series Inc., Hauppauge, New York, 1996.

___. *The New Canary Handbook*, Barron's Educational Series, Inc., Hauppauge, New York, 1992.

___. *The New Bird Handbook*, Barron's Educational Series, Inc., Hauppauge, New York, 1989.

Magazines

Bird Talk
P.O. Box 3940
San Clemente, CA 92672

Journal of the Association of Avian Veterinarians
5770 Lake Worth Road
Lake Worth, FL 33463-3299

The Author

Dr. Otto von Frisch, son of the Nobel prize winner Dr. Karl von Frisch ("Frisch on Bees"), grew up surrounded by every conceivable kind of animal. His tame jackdaw "Tobby" and other birds were his childhood companions.

Professor von Frisch studied biology at Munich University. His doctorate, written in 1956, was on "The Breeding Biology and Early Development of the Curlew." Today he is director of the Natural History Museum in Braunschweig, Germany, and professor at the Technical University of Braunschweig. In 1973 he received the German Children's Book Prize for his *1,000 Tricks with Camouflage*.

The Photographer

Uwe Anders is a first-degree biologist and for many years has been active as a free-lance natural photographer and as a cameraman for nature film productions. He writes articles on nature themes and teaches nature and travel photography.

The Artist

Johann Brandstetter works as a painter, illustrator, and restorer. He regularly travels with biologists to Central Africa and Asia where he works with them as illustrators of plants and animals.

Important Note

Ornithosis (see page 58) is at this time quite rare in canaries, but the disease can give rise to life-threatening conditions in both humans and canaries. For this reason you should take your canary to the avian veterinarian if you suspect it may have contracted the disease, and visit your own doctor if you have cold or flu symptoms. Be sure to tell your doctor that you have a bird.

You can be a born bird lover, but you still need years of experience to become a bird expert. And even a bird expert doesn't hesitate to ask advice and help from an avian veterinarian. If no one with that specialty is available in your immediate area, ask your local bird club members or write to The Association of Avian Veterinarians, 5770 Lake Worth Road, Lake Worth, FL 33463-3299. This organization should be able to recommend a veterinarian who works with birds.

Photos

Photo page 1: Various color mutations; pages 2–3: With its beak open, one bird threatens two others that are approaching the food source; pages 4–5: This ceramic dish is large enough for these canaries to get their plumage really wet; 6–7: The Gloster shows who is the boss! 64–65 (Lettuce should be washed thoroughly as it often has traces of pesticides left in the folds of the leaves.)

First English language edition published in 1999 by Barron's Educational Series, Inc.

Published originally under the title *Kanarienvögel*

All inquiries should be addressed to:
Barron's Educational Series, Inc.
250 Wireless Boulevard
Hauppauge, NY 11788
http://www.barronseduc.com

Library of Congress Catalog Card No. 99-10566

Library of Congress Cataloging-in-Publication Data
Frisch, Otto von.
[Kanarienvogel. English]
Canaries / Otto von Frisch ; photography, Uwe Anders ; illustrations, Johann Brandstetter ; translated and adapted by Matthew M. Vriends.
p. cm. — (A complete pet owner's manual)
Includes bibliographical references and index.
ISBN-13: 978-0-7641-0936-2
ISBN-10: 0-7641-0936-7
1. Canaries. I. Title. II. Series.
SF463.F7513 1999
636.6'8625—dc21 99-10566
CIP

Printed in China
19 18 17 16 15 14 13 12

EXPERT ADVICE

1	**Should I purchase one or two canaries?**	*A canary is happier in the company of other canaries.*
2	**Can I keep two canary males in the same cage or aviary?**	*Generally, canaries live together peacefully, although males can be rather aggressive.*
3	**Do male canaries sing if kept in large cages with other pet birds?**	*Male canaries sing very well in roomy cages or aviaries in the company of other birds.*
4	**What should I do when I want to buy a good singer?**	*If you are interested in an excellent singer, go to a breeder of song canaries.*
5	**Where should I buy canaries?**	*Local canary breeders and reputable pet stores carry many varieties of canaries.*